THE ALHAMBRA AND THE GENERALIFE

Text, photographs, lay-out and reproduction, entirely designed and created by the Technical Department of EDITORIAL ESCUDO DE ORO, S.A.

Editorial Escudo de Oro, S.A.

Part of the Alhambra by night.

The Gate of Justice in a 19th-century engraving. ▷

THE ALHAMBRA

The Alhambra is the finest, best-conserved mediaeval Arab palace in the world; it is also a monument that is intimately associated with the history of Granada and with the city's appearance. Emilio García Gómez, the illustrious Arabist, wrote that "The Alhambra is like an egg, with its relatively hard shell, its delicious yolk and even its white, which the 'cooking' of passing time has left clear in colour. I would like to sustain the metaphor by stating that with these two words, 'white' and 'clear,' I am also opposing the theory that holds the Alhambra to be over-adorned; for there are a lot of flat surfaces, bare walls, right angles and clear spaces in the Moorish palace — in sum, a tremendous 'functional sense of architecture' which the architects of Spain were right to underline, as a model even, in their 'Alhambra Manifesto' (1952)."
The Alhambra stands on a hill to the east of Granada, on the left bank of the Darro, facing the Alcazaba and Albaicín quarters. The famous, artistic monument is enclosed by a ring of walls some 2 km in circumference. Its perimeter is irregular, bounded by the river Darro to the north, by the Assabica valley to the south and by the *Cuesta* (Slope) *del Rey Chico* to the east; the Alhambra's precinct is thus separated,

REAL FORTALEZA
ALHAMBRA

The graceful outline of the Alhambra and the robust Renaissance architecture of the Charles V Palace stand out against the greenery of their surroundings.

The Parade Ground, the Keep and the Broken Tower.

respectively, from the Albaicín, the *Torres Bermejas* ('Vermilion Towers') and the Generalife. The hill on which the palace stands is covered with charming, intense green vegetation — the woods and gardens of the Moorish citadel — thanks to irrigation by water from the Sierra Nevada, distributed by an efficient system of channels.

In the 13th century the founder of the Nazari dynasty, Mohammed ben Al Ahmar, established his residence within the defences afforded by Al-Sabika castle, located on one of Granada's hills. By its side there grew up an aristocratic and administrative city known

Inside the Parade Gate.

The Alhambra against the Sierra Nevada.

The Alhambra and (left) the Charles V Palace.

The Gate of Justice.

Overall view of the Alhambra (pp. 8-9).

The Wine Gate and the fortress towers.

Detail of the Wine Gate.

The Wine Gate leads on to the Cistern Square.

The so-called Machuca gardens.

as the Alhambra ('the red'): this was the beginning of the Alhambra's period of greatest splendour. The greater part of the buildings, as they survive today, date essentially from the reigns of Abul Hachach Yusuf I (1333-1353) and of his son Mohammed V (1353-1391). Very little of what was built by later kings, however, has been retained: scarcely more than the decoration of the *Torre de las Infantas,* dating from the Saadien period (1445-1461).
After Granada was reconquered by the troops of the Catholic Monarchs (Ferdinand and Isabella), the converted Moslem Francisco de las Maderas was commissioned to decorate the Alhambra palaces. They were relatively well cared for during the reigns of the monarchs of the Austria dynasty too; but in the 18th century the Alhambra was lamentably neglected. The monument's deterioration reached its most serious level when it was occupied by French troops. There followed a long period of absolute abandon, until the Alhambra was classified as a National Monument in 1870: thenceforth its definitive falling into ruins was successfully prevented.
The overall precinct of the Alhambra is made up of the Alcazaba (a military fortress at the western extreme); the Royal Palace on the central part of the hill; and the High Alhambra, on the eastern side, which

Entry to the Machuca tower.

Part of the Albaicín.

was inhabited by potentates, civil servants and manufacturers. The contiguous *Torres Bermejas* constitute a fortified outpost of the Alhambra; they were one of the original defences of the ancient city of Granada.

The Alhambra has inspired many poets, and was the subject of the North American Washington Irving's famous *Tales of the Alhambra.* Angel Ganivet, a native of Granada, devoted this admirable poem to the monument:

How still your sleep,
Alhambran towers!
Your dream of Death,
Yet death still far.
With the rising sun
Your walls aglow;
With the moon are kissed
By pallid light.
How still your sleep
With death yet far!
Serene the night
That spangles your sleep,
And the black-winged night
That enfolds you deep.
How still your sleep,
With death yet far!
Your battlements bedecked,
With purest dew.
Cruel, lashing rain
Your solid walls does thrash.
How still your sleep
With death yet far!
A loving breeze
Brings morning's kiss
A mighty wind
At your portals thrums
How still your sleep
With death yet far!
Centuries of sleep
Down your walls do flow,
Flow to your deep,
Then death will come
O were I as you
For centuries to dream
And from dreams to fall
To the shadows of nought!

PUERTA DE LA JUSTICIA

The 'Gate of Justice' is the main entrance to the Alhambra nowadays. It was built during the reign of Yusuf I, and completed in 1348. It is made up of a horseshoe arch opened in the façade, with a brick frame and a voussoired lintel. There is a hand in intaglio on the marble keystone. The archway of the *Puerta de la Justicia* gives onto an open space designed for defensive purposes; beyond this is the inner gate, displaying a voussoired horseshoe arch of stone with scallops on the keystone and spandrels. This archway is supported by short columns with square capitals.

There is an inscription in Arabic characters over the arch; and also, above a broad band of artistic *azulejos* (glazed tiles), a niche with life-size figures of the Virgin and the Child Jesus, sculpted by Roberto

The Mexuar Hall.

Another view of the Mexuar Hall.

Alemán — on instructions from the Catholic Monarchs — in 1500-01. These monarchs' emblems, the yoke and arrows, appear below the statues.
The Arab bolt and latch on the door itself are very interesting. Once through the doorway, the visitor will reach a spacious vestibule comprising three vaulted rooms. The exit door, finally, features a horseshoe arch retaining fine decorative *azulejos* on the left-hand pendentive.

PUERTA DEL VINO

The 'Wine Gate' may have been the entrance to the High Alhambra, the village. The outer façade, the oldest one, displays a pointed horseshoe arch and low voussoirs in relief. Above the archway there is a voussoir lintel with a symbolic key in the centre and, higher up, an inscription in praise of God and Mohammed V.

Detail of mosaic in the Mexuar Hall. ▷

The Mosque court (Mexuar) in a 19th-century engraving.

Capital of one of the columns.

The Mexuar Court: front of the Golden Room.

The Mexuar Court: front of the Comares Hall.

The Golden Room.

View of the Court of Myrtle Trees. ▷

Part of the Court of Myrtle Trees.

Court of Myrtle Trees: detail of the South Door.

Court of Myrtle Trees: detail of the door.

Court of Myrtle Trees seen from the South Door.

Entrance to the Comares Tower through the Court of Myrtle Trees (pp. 24/25).

The Court of Myrtle Trees seen from the Barca Gallery and a detail of the mosaic in the courtyard.

The arch in the inner façade features spendrels adorned with beautiful multicoloured *azulejos.* A voussoir lintel above the archway supports the second storey. There is a Nazari escutcheon at the junction of the two arches, with the following inscription: "Only God is victorious."

The *Plaza de los Aljibes* ('Cisterns Square') is the next section, with the Alcazaba to its left. The Alcazaba and the 'Vermilion Towers' are the oldest buildings in the Alhambra — the fortress was mentioned in documents as early as the 11th century. Building work was concluded in the reign of Mohammed ben Al Ahmar, who also raised the Keep, the *Torre Quebrada* and the *Torre de la Vela.*

Access to the Alcazaba is via the *Plaza de los Aljibes* and the fascinating *Jardín de los Adarves* ('Parapet Walks Garden'). At the western extreme of this garden is the small *Torre de la Pólvora* ('Gunpowder Tower'), from whence one can enter the fortress. In the interior, the Parade Ground is enclosed by ramparts with several towers: the Keep, *Torre del Adarguero* and *Torre Quebrada* are the principal ones.

THE KEEP

The *Torre del Homenaje* — Keep — measures 26 m in height and is made up of five storeys, divided into square rooms separated one from another by buttresses with ground-plan in the shape of a cross, in turn supported by round arches, with different types of vault.

The Keep, one of the most interesting towers in the Alcazaba, was the residence of the fortress's governors in the 16th century.

An old engraving of the Court of Myrtle Trees. ▷

The Court of Myrtle Trees from the upper gallery.

Entry to the Barca Gallery.

A corner in the Ambassadors' Hall.

The Ambassadors' Hall.

Detail of the entry arch to the Barca Gallery.

Detail of the mosaic in the Ambassadors' Hall.

TORRE DE LA VELA

The *Torre de la Vela* comprises four storeys on a sturdy base. This tower was restored so as to convert it into a dwelling: among other alterations, this involved adding the staircase that leads to the upper platform. The large building standing next to the *Torre de la Vela* was apparently used as the stables of the fortress. It is divided into three sections of different sizes by means of brick pillars supporting segmental arches, round arches and barrel vaults dating from the 13th-14th centuries.

TORRE DE LAS ARMAS

The 'Arms Tower', projecting from the lower ramparts of the Alhambra, was built earlier than the 'Tower of Justice'. Access to the city was from here, by means of a path that crossed the woods and led to the bridge of the Cadi (Moslem judge) in Carrera del Darro.
The outer façade displays a horseshoe arch of brick, with stone imposts, adorned by glazed white, blue and green stones. Beyond this archway is another similar one leading to a gallery with a vaulted ceiling.

THE ROYAL PALACES

The Royal Palaces are made up of three separate groups of monuments: the *Mexuar* or *Cuarto Dorado* ('Golden Room'), used for the administration of justice; the *Cuarto de Comares,* official residence of the king; and the *Cuarto de los Leones,* the sovereign's private quarters. The *Cuarto de Comares* displays a pure Arab style, while the *Cuarto de los Leones* was restored — with Christian additions — as a result of Mohammed V's relations with Peter I of Castile.

Entrance to these palaces is via a doorway (opened in 1926) leading to a small patio with a vestibule beyond. The *Mexuar* doorway is in the front wall, with a voussoired plasterwork lintel, eaves supported by carved wooden lintels, and a frieze with an inscription and small escutcheons displaying the Nazaris' device at the sides.

THE MEXUAR

Parts of the *Mexuar* have been demolished: what remains does not give the visitor an exact idea of the palace's original appearance, for — as well as the alterations carried out in the reign of Yusuf I — later, after Granada had been conquered by the Catholic Monarchs, several Christian edifices were built.

View of Granada from the Ambassadors' Hall.

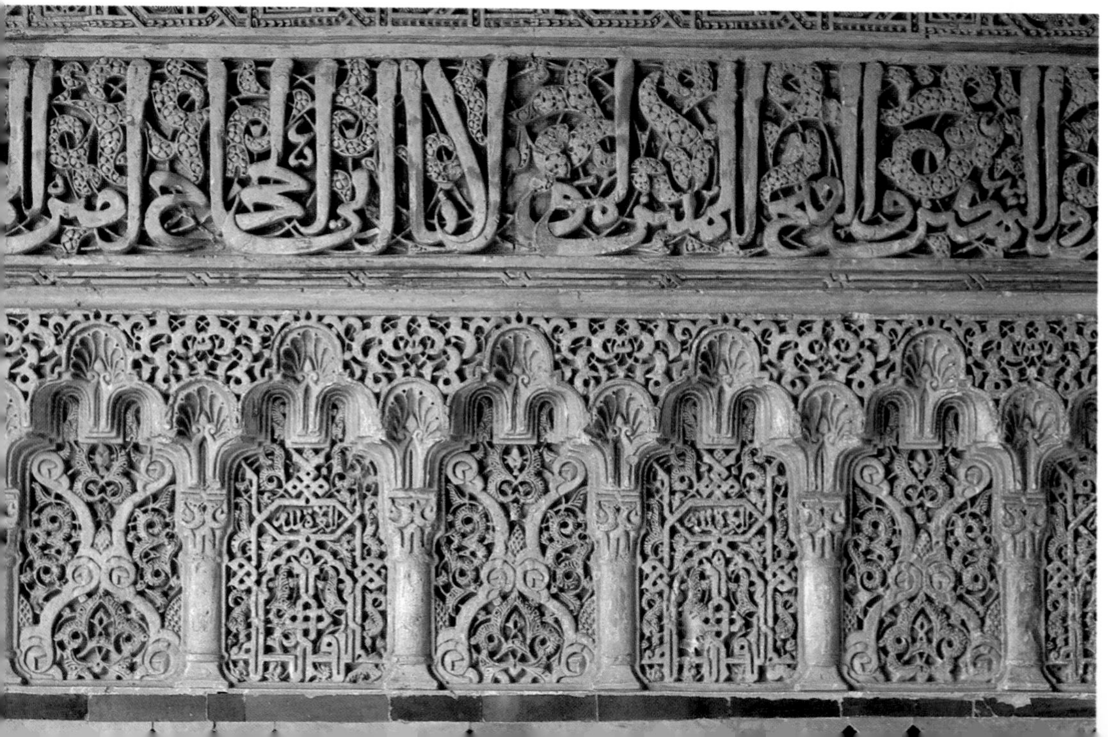

The filigree decoration in the Ambassadors' Hall and a detail of the stuccowork.

MACHUCA'S PATIO

The gardens which today make up Machuca's Patio rest on part of the foundations of earlier building which surrounded the original patio, to which access was afforded by means of a door behind the paved esplanade. Later there was a second square patio with a small pool in the centre and which was flanked by rooms. The only remaining vestige of the whole precinct is the east wing *(Sala del Mexuar)* together with a beautiful portico in the north wall. The portico, restored in 1926, displays nine scalloped arches resting on marble columns. 'Machuca's Tower' is in the centre behind this portico: the architects who built Charles V's Palace resided here.

THE MEXUAR HALL

The interior of the *Mexuar* hall has undergone different alterations; the works executed in 1537-1544 converted it into a chapel. There are four columns forming a square in the centre. Rebuilding work by the Christians included the addition of a panelled ceiling. The upper part of the hall boasts decorative plasterwork, the greater part gilded and painted, similar to

Belvedere of the Ambassadors' Hall.

The Queen's belvedere seen from the Ambassadors' Hall.

The Lions' Court with its central fountain.

Detail of the Lions' Court. ▷

that in the hall of the Generalife. Other very interesting items include the bands of glazed tiles with the Nazaris' device, Charles V's coat of arms, the Mendoza family escutcheon, the panels depicting the Pillars of Hercules, and a frieze with interlaced Moorish designs, all dating from the 16th century.
At the back of the room there is a mirador-cumoratory, restored in 1917, dominating beautiful views of the valley of the Darro from its four small balconies. This fine mirador displays superb decoration and a voussoired horseshoe arch featuring various texts — maxims from the Koran and extolments of Mohammed V.

THE MEXUAR PATIO

This courtyard lies between the walls of the *Mexuar* and those of the Comares Palace. The *Cuarto Dorado,* a part of the Comares Palace built in the time of Mohammed V, gives onto the north side. It is preceded by a portico made up of three arches supported by columns with marble capitals, dating from the 12th or 13th century. A small horseshoe arch on the left leads to the *Mexuar.* There is also a larger one beyond, with scallops and hinge-posts decorated with *mocárabes* (designs of interlaced prisms), surmounted by two lattices and flanked by two smaller

The foutain of the Lions' Court.

The Lions' Court. ▷

archways: the three afford access to a gallery adorned by a panelled ceiling with interlaced designs, Gothic paintings, the coats of arms of the Catholic Monarchs, and the yoke and arrows.

THE COMARES PALACE

Abutted by the Court of Myrtle Trees, the Comares Palace, like the Comares Tower, looks out towards the Darro Valley. Work on the Palace was begun in the reign of Youssef I and continued by his son Mohammed V who provided it with a fine front (opposite the doorway of the Golden Room in the Mexuar Court). This front has a pair of symmetric lintelled doors surrounded by delightful glazed tile-work topped by voussoired plasterwork lintels; the whole rests on a ceramic-work dado. On the upper of this front there are twin windows with stilted festoonry arches; another, smaller, window has a lobulated arch and is bordered by a ceramic-work inscription. The richly-decorated wall bears inscriptions of praise to Allah and Mohammed V. Also of interest are the friezes, one in stalagtite, and another, richly-worked, which serves as a corniche. The large eave covering the frieze is also done in worked wood.

Columns in the Lions' Court.

Corner of the Lions' Court.

PATIO DE LOS ARRAYANES

There is a pool in the centre of this courtyard, with a modern marble fountain at either end. The patio is in the Andalusian Arabic style, flanked by two series of rooms and with porticoes of seven round arches at the ends. The ceiling of the southern gallery is covered with interlaced designs, and also seven small domes of different shapes; the gallery has an alcove at either end. There is a large semicircular arch in the centre of the façade, with three lattices and a modern door.

Above this portico stretches a passageway with seven windows giving onto the courtyard. The windows were restored in the Christian period and feature Gothic capitals and modern lattices. Over the passageway, in turn, there is a vast gallery with interlaced designs on the ceiling, with six archways and a lintelled opening in the centre supported by twin layered struts of wood.

There is a crenellated parapet with two small towers (raised in modern times) at the sides, above the gallery on the north side (behind which stands Comares tower). At each end of this gallery is an alcove with arches decorated with ovoli and domes and shelves adorned with interlaced designs. The socle of *azulejos* opposite the portico is an interesting sight:

A 19th-century engraving of the Lions' Court.

The fountain of the Lions' Court (pp. 40/41).

The Lions' Court.

Detail of the columns in the Lions' Court.

View of the Courtyard of the Lions.

Nineteenth-century engraving of the Abencerrajes Gallery.

Decoration of the Abencerrajes Gallery ceiling.

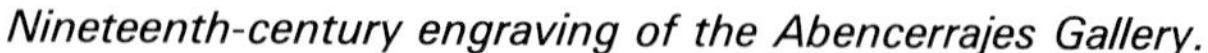

this is an imitation Arab work executed by Antonio Tenorio and Gaspar Hernández from 1587 to 1599. There is an inscription in plaster above the socle, a fragment of the qasidah that Ben Zemrec wrote in honour of Mohammed V.

SALA DE LA BARCA

The *Sala de la Barca* is located to the north of the *Patio de los Arrayanes;* one enters through a pointed arch with *mocárabes* (interlaced prisms), the spandrels adorned with designs of foliage and pinecones. The jambs of this arch feature niches with small marble archways, the interior decorated with ceramics of geometrical design. The artistic semicylindrical vault of the *Sala de la Barca* was partially destroyed by fire in 1890. The plasterwork mouldings on the walls display the Nazari coat of arms. The arch in the middle is flanked by two alcoves with traces of a poetic inscription around them.

The Abencerrajes Gallery.

Paintings on the ceiling of the Kings' Hall.

THE COMARES TOWER AND AMBASSADORS' HALL

The height (45 metres) and thickness of the walls (2.5 metres) remind us that the Comares Tower is the Alhambra's strongest and was conceived as a military building.
Inside the tower stands the Comares or Ambassadors' Hall, built by Youssef I. This was the centre of political life and the venue for diplomacy and negotiations, since it was in this hall that the throne stood.
The name of Comares Hall comes from the stained glass windows; *Comares* is a corruption of the name of these windows *(qamariyyas* or *comarías)* in Arabic. The hall measures 11.3 metres square by 18.2 metres high. The flooring was originally in marble and a fountain must once have occupied the centre, as in the remaining salons. Today there is an alternation of clay tiles and late 16th-century glazed-tile flooring with the Alahmar coat-of-arms.
The great number of apertures in the shape of doors, windows and balconies (of which there are nine) is a determining factor in the decoration of the walls. The *alicatado* (glazed mosaic) dado, the intricacy of the stucco-work and the extraordinary detail of the tracery on the cedarwood ceiling (still preserving some of its colouring) are reminders of the former splendour of this magnificent court. Ornamental motifs are the characteristic epigraphs, *ataurique* (plasterwork with leaf and flower motifs) work and geometrical figures. The hall is a veritable gem, built with masterly skill and attention to detail.
In former times sunlight was dimmed by thick curtains, splendid plaster lattice windows and elegant *ajimeces* (jutting wooden belvederes with coloured glass), giving the ensemble an air of mystery, very much in Oriental taste.

THE LIONS' PALACE

This palace was built by Mohammed V as royal private apartments and is located in the corner formed by the baths and the Comares courtyard, with which it forms a perpendicular axis. It is a splendid example of Granada Islamic art. Access to it is via a narrow corridor lingking the Court of Myrtle Trees with the Lions' Palace. The Lions' Palace comprises a large central courtyard surrounded by galleries, with large salons at the far end. To the north stands the Hall of the Two Sisters and behind it the Ajimeces Hall as well as the Mirador de Daraxa; to the south the Abencerrajes Hall with the Harem; to the east the Kings' Hall and to the west the Mocarabes Hall.

A 19th-century engraving of the Kings' Hall.

The Hall of Justice in an old engraving.

THE MOCARABES HALL

This hall is an elongated rectangle with intricately-worked plasterwork bands bearing religious inscriptions as well as the Nazrid coat-of-arms and motto. The original vault (uncovered in the 19th century and adjacent to the 17th-century vault) is of great interest. By means of three arches decorated with *mocarabes* (a term referring to stalagtite stucco or wood work, and giving the hall its name) supported on half-columns and capitals bearing inscriptions of praise to Mohammed V, access to the Lions' Court is afforded.

PATIO DE LOS LEONES

The name of the 'Court of Lions' is due to the twelve figures of lions supporting the fountain in its centre. This courtyard is rectangular and enclosed by a gallery of 124 elegant white marble columns with cylindrical shafts, ringed towards the top, supporting square capitals with large abaci; above these there are pillars of brick displaying plasterwork decoration and supporting plinths that bear the roof and an artistic carved wooden frieze with the Nazari device. The

The Kings' Hall, otherwise known as the Hall of Justice.

Entry to the Hall of the Two Sisters.

eaves we see today are a 19th-century copy of the original roof.

The centre arches on the long sides of the courtyard are round, with *mocárabes* in the archivolts and plasterwork with foliage designs in the spandrels. A decorated plasterwork frieze runs along the top of the walls of the courtyard, with inscriptions in praise of God and the sovereign.

The white marble Fountain of Lions is one of the most beautiful, perfect specimens of the Arabic school of sculpture in Granada. Amidst the decorative floral motifs on the rim of the basin there is an inscription with a fragment of the qasidah dedicated to Mohammed V by Aben Zemrec. The basin of the fountain rests, by means of short turned balusters, on the backs of the twelve statues of lions (sculpted in an archaic style) that form a circle and spout water from their mouths.

The cloister-shape arrangement of the 28.5 by 15.7 metre Lions' Court (Patio de los Leones) places it outside the mainstream of typical Moslem Andalusian courts.

Half-way along the shorter galleries there are two small temples or pavilions jutting out towards the court. Inside the pavilions are semi-spherical wooden ceilings with intricate interlacing-arch work, a magnificent example of the the consummate skill of the Arab carpenters in Granada. Curiously enough, these pavilions are somewhat similar to the small temples of the cloisters in some of Spain's Cistercian monasteries.

Although the eye-catching colouring has been lost with the passing of time and the vagaries of history, the Lions' Court still preserves its incredibly harmonious and elegant architecture intact.

Detail of the fine coffering in the Hall of the Two Sisters.

The Hall of the Two Sisters in a 19th-century engraving.

Detail of the mosaic in the Hall of the Two Sisters.

THE HAREM

The only remaining vestiges of the Harem are the courtyard and the sections by the main walls, which were restored in 1924. In the courtyard there are two porticoes, each consisting of three arches supported by columns. The walls display decorative stripes, a frieze of frescoes, and carved eaves.

SALA DE LOS ABENCERRAJES

The 'Hall of the Abencerrages' is opposite the *Sala de las Dos Hermanas.* Its name is a consequence of the legend according to which the chiefs of the Abencerrage dynasty were massacred here. Entrance is via a double archway; the central part of the room is square, with three pairs of artistically decorated arches supported by columns with blue capitals. The lavish ornamentation of the walls was restored in the 16th century; and the cupola, adorned with *mocárabes,* is particularly beautiful.

SALA DE LOS REYES

The 'Hall of Kings' is also known as the *Sala de la Justicia,* or 'Hall of Justice'. It forms a rectangular section measuring 31 m by 7 m, to the east of the Court of Lions. Access to the Hall is via three porticoes of three arches decorated by *mocárabes,* supported by slender columns and adorned with openwork rhombi. The interior of the 'Hall of Kings' is divided into three square sections separated one from another by pairs of sturdy arches. The rectangles formed by these arches are enclosed by vaults adorned with interlaced designs. There are a number of alcoves at the ends of the Hall, decorated with inscriptions extolling God and Mohammed V. The ensemble of the interior of the 'Hall of Justice' is in fact one of the most attractive in the whole of the Alhambra. The ceilings are adorned with remarkable paintings; in the centre are the figures of ten Arab personages conversing, on a golden background with relief decorations and coats of arms held by lions. This is apparently a depiction of the first ten sultans of the Nazari dynasty; the paintings may well date from the late 14th and early 15th centuries.

These vividly-coloured and simply sketched pictures bring to mind the techniques of Chinese drawings and Persian manuscript miniatures. The similarity of preparation and execution between these pictures and those found in Barbary, and above all Morocco, provides strong evidence of Moorish influence. It is interesting to note that these paintings were executed on animal hides sewn together, then adhered to the wooden vaulting.

The Hall of the Two Sisters, decorated with stuccowork, with the Ajimeces Gallery.

The fine stuccowork in the Daraxa Belvedere.

HALL OF THE TWO SISTERS

This 8-metre-square hall was probably built towards the end of the reign of Mohammed V. Its name (Sala de las Dos Hermanas) derives from the large twin marble slabs set in the flooring flanking a central fountain.

The hall has half-point arches at each end. The side arches afford access to two small rooms with interlaced-design ceilings.

The walls are covered in extremely intricate filigree-like plasterwork representing various motifs, though most of them are typical of the second half of the 14th century. The alicatado-work on the dado with its metallic irisdiscence is of great interest; some of the glazing is done in such striking colours as violet.

The most impressive part of the hall is the stalagtite dome. It looks like a weightless vault floating in space as if by magic. The dome rests on an octagonal base, on squinches again decorated with stalagtite-work.

The upper apartments were in all likelihood reserved for the women who, behind their wooden lattice windows, watched the entertainment and festivities without themselves being seen.

The poetic Daraxa Belvedere in a 19th-century engraving. ▷

SALA DE LOS AJIMECES

This room's name derives from the two small balconies, or *ajimeces,* that give onto the garden from the north wall. The ceiling, with a design of interlaced prisms, was restored by Francisco de las Maderas, a converted Moslem, from 1537 to 1541. Half of the walls are covered in plasterwork with religious inscriptions and a small shield with the Nazari device.
A large pointed arch with *mocárabes* in the centre of the rear wall of the *Sala de los Ajimeces* affords access to 'Daraxa's Balcony', a superb work of Arab art.

THE MIRADOR DE DARAXA

"I-ain-dar-aixa" ("Eyes of the Sultana"), the name of this belvedere, would seem to show that it was built for the Sultana to contemplate the beauty of the countryside stretching as far as the Darro valley, before the apartments of Charles V were built. The windows are very low, since the Arab custom was to sit on cushions on the floor.
Wall decoration is of unbelievable intricacy and unsurpassed beauty, comparable to the finest and most delicate work in ivory. Most of the epigraphs are taken from the Arab poet Aben Zemrec.
The inside of the belvedere is taken up by a small rectangular room with two side arches and a double arch at the front. The window-recesses are stalagtite-decorated pointed arches.
The magnificent and intricately-decorated tilework dado is a combination of black, white and yellow. The dado is topped by a small, alicatado-work inscription. The wooden coffer-work of the panelled ceiling was originally combined with coloured glass, which has now been replaced.

The Daraxa Belvedere.

The fountain of the Daraxa Garden.

CHARLES V'S ROOMS

Charles V's Rooms, located between the *Peinador de la Reina,* the rampart, and the baths, were built in 1527. The ensemble of the six rooms displays Renaissance decoration. The first two rooms feature fine wooden ceilings with square panels; Washington Irving lived in the other four.

THE DARAXA GARDEN

Adjacent to the Baths' north doorway and with a gallery intervening stands the Cypress (or Grille) Court and the romantic Daraxa Garden. The south front of this garden is bounded by the Hall of the Two Sisters and the Mirador de Daraxa. In the centre of the garden in the Daraxa Court stands a large marble fountain; this fountain once stood in the Mexuar Court and was moved to its present site in 1626. The basement of the Hall of the Two Sisters comprises a series of vaulted galleries built around the so-called Hall of Secrets.

ABUL HACHACH'S TOWER

Abul Hachach's Tower stands on a rectangular ground-plan and backs onto the Royal Palace. The room is divided by two columns; on each side there

Court of the Cypresses (also known as Court of the Grille).

are three balconies with plasterwork arches and, on the sills, vestiges of fine glazed tiles with inscriptions. This tower was decorated by Yusuf I and modified by Mohammed V.

Further alterations in 1538 gave rise to a room, surrounded by galleries, that was named the *Peinador de la Reina* ('Queen's Toilette'). The gallery is made up of seven stilted arches; the *Peinador* is rectangular in shape and conserves nine round Arabic arches which have been altered. The room also displays frescoes painted from 1539 to 1546 by Giulio de Aquiles and Alexander Mayner, pupils of Raphael or of Giovanni da Udine.

View of the Hall of Rest.

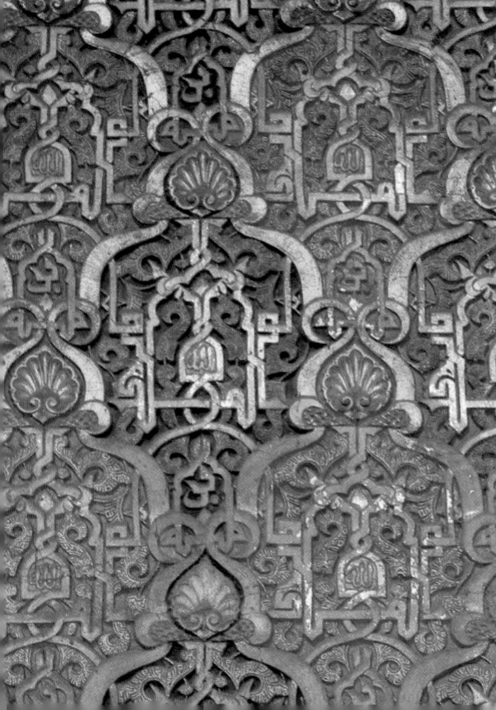

Details of the Hall of Rest and the stuccowork inside.

Detail of the upper part of the Hall of Rest and its fine ceiling.

The Baths.

THE BATHS

The baths are situated to the east of Comares Palace; their disposition is reminiscent of that of Roman thermal baths. The *Sala de las Camas* features four columns supporting corbels and lintels and delimiting a square area with a fountain in the centre and surrounded by galleries. The walls are covered with lavishly colourful decoration. Most of the creations here date from the Christian period. The paving was made by Francisco de las Maderas, in Isabel de Robles' pottery, from 1541 to 1542.

From this first room one can gain access to the interior of the baths, presenting a superb architectural style, the walls unadorned. The baths display white marble floors, friezes of azulejos, flat horse-shoe arches, and tunnel vaults with stellar skylights. A stilted arch gives access to the central room.

Corner of the fine access stairway to the Baths. ▷

DETAILS OF THE ALHAMBRA PALACE

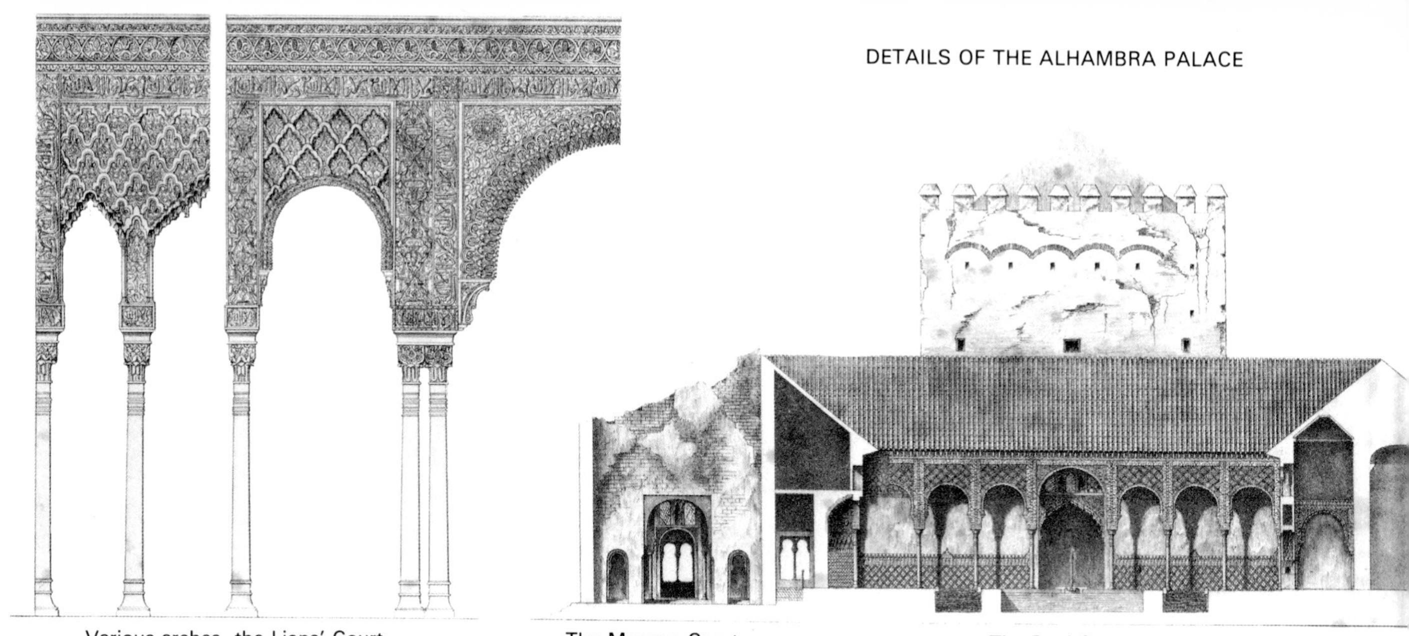

Various arches, the Lions' Court

The Mosque Court

The Pool Court

The Ambassadors' Hall

The Antechamber

The Pool Court

The old Arab baths

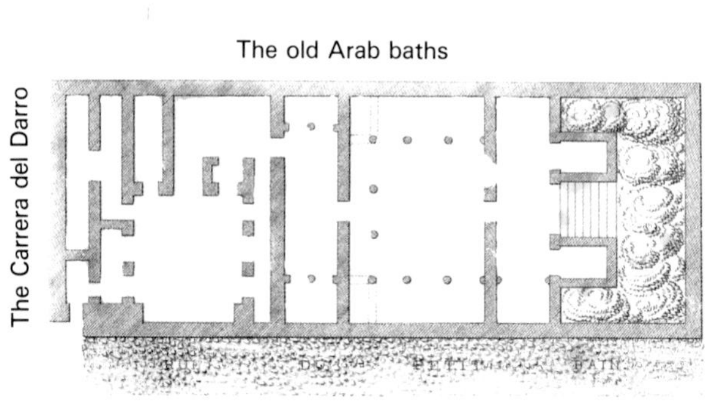

The Gate of Justice

The Lions' Court The Hall of Justice Various arches, the Pool Court

The Hall of the Two Sisters The Lions' Court The Abencerrajes Gallery Baths. The Rest Hall

The Wine Gate

The Infantas' Tower

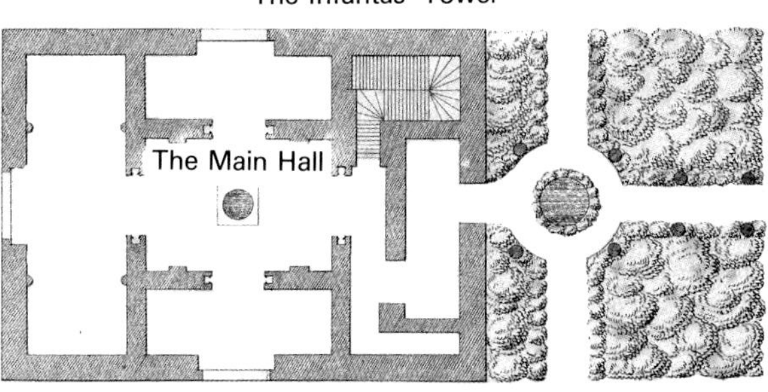

1
9
2
3
4
5
7
8
6

Christian-Moorish houses in the Partal.

DIVERSE DETAILS OF THE ALHAMBRA.
1. Arch in the west gallery of the Lions' Court. - 2. Frieze. - 3. Fragment of a window near the Infantas' Boudoir. - 4. Arab bas-relief, the only one in Granada. Though the surrounding inscription is badly worn, from the nature of the letters it is thought to be 14th century. - 5. Mosaics in the Ambassadors' Hall. - 6. The Lions' Fountain: height from the ground to the upper crown is 2.13 metres; diameter of the main basin is 2.51. - 7. One of the lions of the fountain: its head stands 85 cm from the ground. - 8. Capitals in the Arab Baths. - 9. Lozenge decoration in the spaces above the arches in the Lions' Court.

The Partal.

General view of the Partal gardens.

TORRE DE LAS DAMAS

The 'Ladies' Tower', behind the *Partal* gardens, was restored from 1920 to 1924. It comprises a portico, a square room behind, and a stairway to the left of the gallery leading to the mirador. The two figures of seated lions, at each side of the portico, are of great interest; they are thought to date from the 10th century. The room itself has three windows in each wall and boasts fine ornamentation, with inscriptions of poems praising God and extolling the building of the Tower. There are also very interesting Arab paintings, which were discovered in 1907.

Ladies' Tower and the Partal Gardens. ▷

THE MIHRAB TOWER

The Mihrab Tower, standing to the right of the *Torre de las Damas,* displays a horseshoe arch in its façade. A round arch supported by columns divides the interior into two sections of different sizes. The Mihrab (niche showing the direction of Mecca), on a polygonal ground-plan, is in the far wall, with a voussoired horseshoe arch and dome decorated with interlaced designs.

OTHER TOWERS IN THE ALHAMBRA

The battlement peaks give the Tower of Peaks (Torre de los Picos) its name; its Gothic design almost makes it seem be work of a 14th-century Christian architect. There are modillions on the corners which no doubt must have once supported watch-towers. The tower has three floors, the third containing a room with a curious Gothic vault. Its purpose was to defend the entrance to the alcazaba (citadel) which com-

In the Partal gardens.

Doorway of the Tower of the Ladies. ▷

The window of the oratory of the Mihrab.

◁ *The Partal against the mountains of Granada (pp. 72/73).*

The Mihrab.

Tower of Peaks with the Generalife in the background.

The Captive's Tower. ▷

◁ *The Infantas' Tower.*

Towers in the Alhambra precinct, after a 19th-century engraving. In the foreground, right, the Tower of the Seven Floors.

municated with the Generalife. The Cadí Tower has a main room (4.45 by 3.4 metres) with a pointed sail vault dating from the times of Youssef I, although it was restored in 1924.

The Captive's Tower (Torre de la Cautiva) is so-called because, according to the legend, D.ª Isabel de Solís, the favourite of King Moulay Hacem, inhabited it. It was used as accommodation by the Christian governors, and then passed into private hands until 1873. The court decoration is of fine stuccowork, and that of the room is reminiscent of the Comares Hall. The alicatado dados are little short of perfect in execution and in the colour combination of purple/rose — a highly original mixture.

The Tower of the Infantas (Torre de las Infantas) is more interesting for its legends than its architecture, since decoration dates from the 15th century, when Granada Arab art was in full decline, and was restored in later years.

Nonetheless it is a very interesting example of an aristocratic Arab dwelling. The legend of the three princesses (Zaida, Zoraida and Zorahaida) who lived here has been immortalised by Washington Irving in his *Tales of the Alhambra*.

The door of the Tower of the Seven Floors (Torre de los Siete Suelos) was the most important one in the Alhambra. Legend has it that it was through this door that the Moorish king Boabdil passed to surrender to the Catholic Monarchs, and having done so asked that it be walled up for ever.

Garden of the Generalife (19th-century engraving).

Gardens of the Generalife.

The name is a reference to the several-storeyed bastion which housed the artillery pieces, as well as to the popular belief that it has seven underground floors — though only two have been discovered so far.

The legends told by P. Echevarría and Washington Irving have made the name of this tower immortal.

In 1812 the tower was blown up by Napoleonic troops and later restored.

THE GENERALIFE

This strategically placed vantage-point on the *Cerro del Sol* or 'Hill of the Sun' was a country house used by the Arab sovereigns of Granada. It is surrounded by splendid gardens where cypress-trees and hedges of laurel, myrtle and orange-bushes abound, and also installed with brilliantly designed fountains. Santiago Rusiñol described the Generalife thus: "One opens a

Overall view of the Pool Court.

The Generalife: the Pool Court.

little door and, on entering the enclosure, an inexplicable aroma, an atmosphere laden with poetry, the tinkling of water dancing on stone, a breeze that makes the leaves sigh and sing, the sight of the flowers, an indefinable quality transmitted by vibrations of light, wrapped in modulated harmony, leaves the visitor bewildered, enables him to enjoy this marvel, and opens the doors to his avid senses."

The Generalife was built around the middle of the 13th century. The ornamentation we see today dates from 1319; it was carried out in the time of Abul Walid Ismail and represents the immediate forerunner of the style characteristic of the Alhambra. Very little of the original building has survived, so that both the structure and the decoration of the present-day edifice date from Abul Walid Ismail's time, with the alterations executed later, after the Catholic Monarchs had reconquered Granada.

The old entrance to the Generalife is in the *Cuesta* (or *Barranco) del Rey Chico,* opposite the Alhambra's *Puerta de Hierro.* Nowadays, however, one enters near the *Torre del Agua,* at the end of the path running along the south wall of the Alhambra.

The Fountain Court in the Generalife. North Porch.

Gardens of the Generalife.

PATIO DE LA ACEQUIA

This patio, measuring 48.7 m by 12.8 m, is the most interesting part of the Generalife. A pool stretches along the centre, flanked on either side by fountains, with stone basins for fountains at each end. The building on the eastern side, which has now been converted into a single room, was raised in the 16th century. On the opposite side there is a wall with eighteen pointed arches affording access to a modern gallery which gives onto the lower gardens. The yoke and arrows are painted on the inside surfaces of the arches; there are also Arabic and Christian inscriptions. Through the centre arch and a fine doorway with ornamental plasterwork one can reach a mirador with three lavishly decorated arches on each side.

THE PAVILIONS

There is a pavilion closing each end of the patio; the southern one is the more interesting, but only five arches supported by brick pillars, and two columns with square capitals, have survived. A small arch with a wavy pattern on the intrados stands on each side of this pavilion: the arch on the right gives access to the main entrance, while the other leads to the stairway climbing to the upper floor. Beyond the colonnade the visitor will come upon a vestibule with two plasterwork arches giving onto a large room retaining traces of its original ornamentation on the walls.
The upper floor is made up of a long hall with alcoves at the ends, with a roof with rafters and collar-beams and also featuring Moorish paintings. There are five

View of the Generalife gardens.

The Alhambra seen from the Generalife.

small balconies opening onto the south side, another in the west wall, and two double arches with small columns flanking the central archway — on the north side — which gives access to a mirador built in recent times.

The north pavilion was enlarged in 1494; with two storeys in the main building, and other sections, it comprises the principal nucleus of the palace. The five arches of the portico display openwork plaster rhombs in the pendentives and are supported by marble columns with square capitals. The ceiling is adorned with intertwined designs, octagonal motifs, stars and *mocárabes.* There is an alcove on either side of the portico.

Three artistic round arches, profusely ornamented and supported by columns with capitals featuring interlaced designs in the classical style of Granada, give access to the room. This portico is surmounted by five small windows with plaster lattices; and there are two recesses, with lintels and decorative inscriptions, in the jambs of the arches.

There are a number of alcoves at the sides of the room, featuring arches and imposts decorated with *mocárabes;* above is a panelled ceiling with interlaced

The Fountain Court. South Porch.

View of the Alhambra from the Generalife.

designs and Arab paintings. There are also small windows with plaster lattices, and alcoves on either side of the portico. The main wall features three arches, with small balconies at the sides, and a larger one in the centre leading to a mirador tower; all these works date from the alterations of 1319. The room in the mirador displays artistic interlaced arches and friezes with the Nazari device in several places. Below the mirador are sixteen small windows with openwork lattices. The walls are exquisitely decorated; in the centre of each window is a balcony with arches giving onto the beautiful, poetic garden below.

A stairway to the left of the room leads up to the sections built in 1494. From the right-hand side one can reach the 'Patio of Cypresses', with several splendid cypress-trees that are hundreds of years old.

On the north side of the 'Patio of Cypresses' there is a two-storeyed gallery, built from 1584 to 1586. In the centre of the patio is a fine pool with small islands covered in luxuriant vegetation with, in the middle, a small stone fountain.

From this patio a broad, sturdy flight of steps dating from the 19th century leads to the upper part of the gardens, a fascinating ensemble of trees and plants.

Next to the upper gallery the visitor will see one of the most beautiful stairways in the Generalife gardens, in the Arab style, under a dense natural vault of laurels and hazel-trees. It is made up of three long, simple flights of steps, each with a landing adorned by a small basin with a fountain in the centre. The stairway is flanked by handrails in the form of channels down which water runs and tinkles musically.

Everything in the Generalife — the patios, gardens and palace — is as if shrouded in a subtle aura of poetry. The charming little palace with its reflection in the pool constitutes a superb scene, full of artistic qualities. The name Generalife apparently derives from the Arabic *Gennat-Alarif,* which means 'Gardens of the Master-Builder'.

The gardens are laid out in a very original manner,

Aerial view of Charles V's palace.

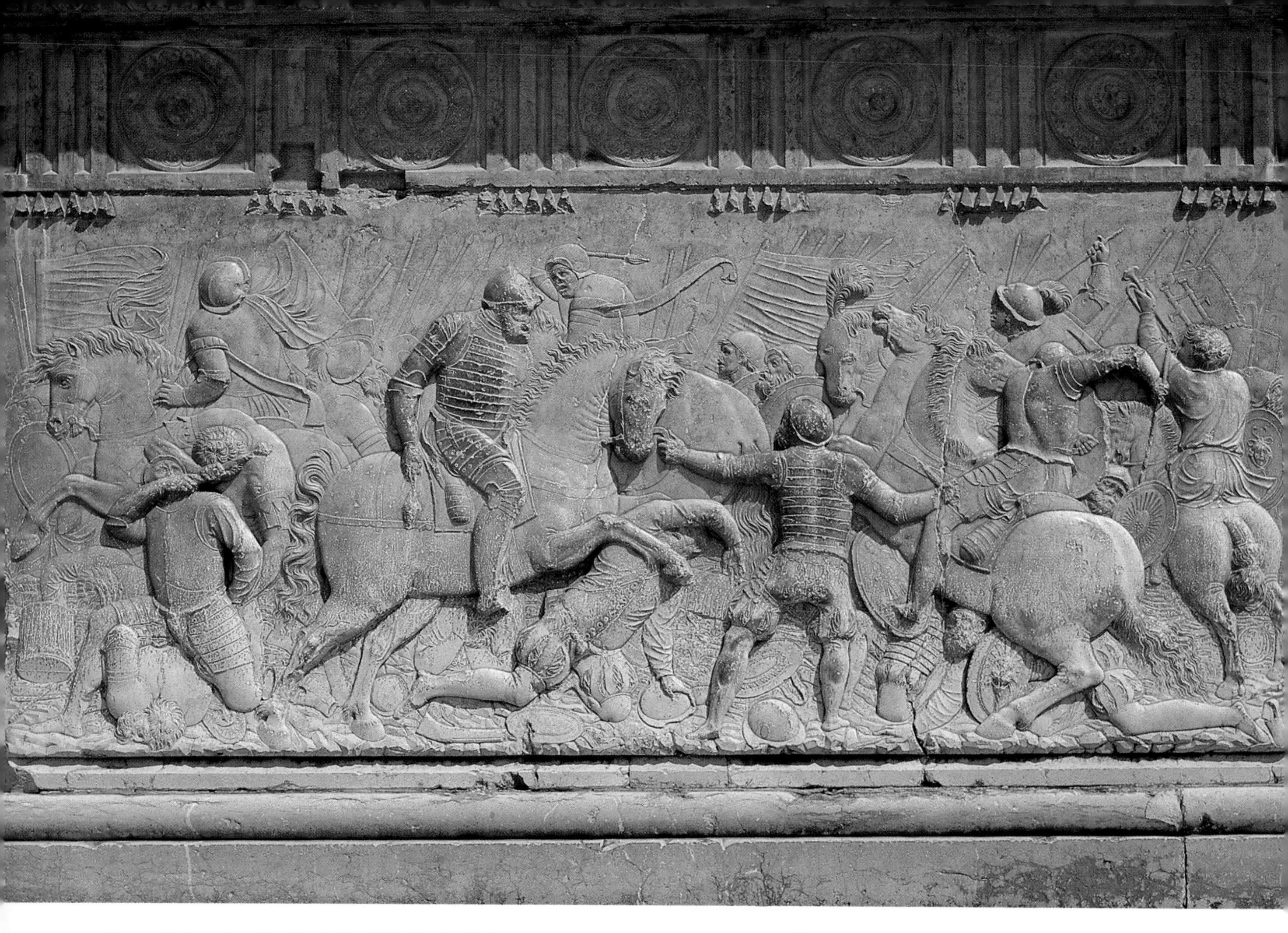

Bas-relief on the front of the Charles V Palace.

making up an attractive ensemble of arbours, flowerbeds with different species (in particular carnations and geraniums, impregnating the air with a simultaneously soft and pervasive scent), delightful fountains, and solid hedges — predominantly of box-trees and noble, melancholy cypresses.
The Generalife is located on a privileged site, from which one can enjoy superb, broad panoramas.

CHARLES V'S PALACE

The Emperor Charles V decided to establish one of his residences at Granada and ordered the construction of a more comfortable palace than the Arab building, equipped for winter. He desired that the new palace be connected to the Alhambra, however, so that he might enjoy the delights of the monument.
Building work on Charles V's Palace began in 1527, under the direction of Pedro Machuca; it had to be suspended in 1568, as a result of the revolt of the Moriscos, and was not resumed until 1579.
The edifice, in the Renaissance style, stands on a quadrangular ground-plan. The balanced majesty of its architectural lines is outstanding: this is considered to be the finest Renaissance palace extant outside Italy.

The originally-designed circular court in the Charles V Palace.

The south front of the Charles V Palace.

Charles V Pillar Fountain. ▷

The most outstanding sights in the exterior are the south front, featuring a very beautiful doorway artistically adorned by Nicolao da Corte, the sculptor, and the magnificent reliefs by Juan de Orea in the west façade.

The large, circular patio in the centre is enclosed by a spacious colonnade supported by Doric columns. The upper gallery, however, is made up of Ionic columns. The National Museum of Spanish-Moslem Art is housed on the ground floor of Charles V's Palace; its collections constitute a highly valuable ensemble of Arab and Mudejar items. The most famous piece is the fascinatingly beautiful Vase of the Alhambra, which was formerly exhibited in the 'Hall of the Two Sisters' for a considerable period of time. Another article of great artistic merit is an 11th-century stone basin, adorned with splendid reliefs depicting lions and antelopes fighting under a tree. The interesting works enriching this Museum also include a beautiful plate from Medina Elvira showing a bird riding a horse; two engraved, embossed gold-plated bracelets; a collection of Visigothic pieces — bracelets, bronze and silver earrings, artistic necklaces of glass and amber, rings, Corinthian capitals; Arab ceramics; and arches, tombs and capitals dating from various different periods.

Carved stone basin, one of the most valuable pieces in the museum of Hispano-Muslim art in Charles V's palace.

The Alhambra jar, which can be admired in the museum of Hispano-Muslim art in Granada.

Contents

Collection ALL EUROPE

		Spanish	French	English	German	Italian	Catalan	Dutch	Swedish	Portuguese	Japanese	Finnish
1	ANDORRA	●	●	●	●	●	●					
2	LISBON	●	●	●	●	●				●		
3	LONDON	●	●	●	●	●					●	
4	BRUGES	●	●	●	●	●		●				
5	PARIS	●	●	●	●	●					●	
6	MONACO	●	●	●	●	●						
7	VIENNA	●	●	●	●	●						
11	VERDUN	●	●	●	●			●				
12	THE TOWER OF LONDON	●	●	●	●							
13	ANTWERP	●	●	●	●	●		●				
14	WESTMINSTER ABBEY	●	●	●	●	●						
15	THE SPANISH RIDING SCHOOL IN VIENNA	●	●	●	●	●						
16	FATIMA	●	●	●	●	●				●		
17	WINDSOR CASTLE	●	●	●	●	●					●	
19	COTE D'AZUR	●	●	●	●	●						
22	BRUSSELS	●	●	●	●	●		●				
23	SCHÖNBRUNN PALACE	●	●	●	●	●		●				
24	ROUTE OF PORT WINE	●	●	●	●	●				●		
26	HOFBURG PALACE	●	●	●	●	●						
27	ALSACE	●	●	●	●	●		●				
31	MALTA		●	●	●	●						
32	PERPIGNAN		●									
33	STRASBOURG	●	●	●	●	●						
34	MADEIRA + PORTO SANTO		●	●	●					●		
35	CERDAGNE - CAPCIR		●				●					
36	BERLIN	●	●	●	●	●						

Collection ART IN SPAIN

		Spanish	French	English	German	Italian	Catalan	Dutch	Swedish	Portuguese	Japanese	Finnish
1	PALAU DE LA MUSICA CATALANA	●		●			●					
2	GAUDI	●	●	●	●	●					●	
3	PRADO MUSEUM I (Spanish Painting)	●	●	●	●	●					●	
4	PRADO MUSEUM II (Foreign Painting)	●	●	●	●	●					●	
5	MONASTERY OF GUADALUPE	●										
6	THE CASTLE OF XAVIER	●	●	●	●						●	
7	THE FINE ARTS MUSEUM OF SEVILLE	●	●	●	●	●						
8	SPANISH CASTLES	●	●	●	●							
9	THE CATHEDRALS OF SPAIN	●	●	●	●							
10	THE CATHEDRAL OF GIRONA	●	●	●	●		●					
11	GRAN TEATRO DEL LICEO	●	●	●			●					
11	EL LICEO ARDE DE NUEVO	●					●					
12	THE CATHEDRAL OF CORDOBA	●	●	●	●	●						
13	THE CATHEDRAL OF SEVILLE	●	●	●	●	●						
14	PICASSO	●	●	●	●	●					●	
15	REALES ALCAZARES (ROYAL PALACE OF SEVILLE)	●	●	●	●	●						
16	MADRID'S ROYAL PALACE	●	●	●	●	●						
17	ROYAL MONASTERY OF EL ESCORIAL	●	●	●	●	●						
18	THE WINES OF CATALONIA	●										
19	THE ALHAMBRA AND THE GENERALIFE	●	●	●	●	●						
20	GRANADA AND THE ALHAMBRA	●										
21	ROYAL ESTATE OF ARANJUEZ	●	●	●	●	●						
22	ROYAL ESTATE OF EL PARDO	●	●	●	●	●						
23	ROYAL HOUSES	●	●	●	●	●						
24	ROYAL PALACE OF SAN ILDEFONSO	●	●	●	●	●						
25	HOLLY CROSS OF THE VALLE DE LOS CAIDOS	●	●	●	●	●						
26	OUR LADY OF THE PILLAR OF SARAGOSSA	●	●	●		●						
27	TEMPLE DE LA SAGRADA FAMILIA	●	●	●	●	●	●					
28	POBLET ABTEI	●	●	●	●		●					
29	MAJORCA CATHEDRAL	●	●	●	●	●	●					

Collection ALL SPAIN

		Spanish	French	English	German	Italian	Catalan	Dutch	Swedish	Portuguese	Japanese	Finnish
1	ALL MADRID	●	●	●	●	●					●	
2	ALL BARCELONA	●	●	●	●	●	●				●	
3	ALL SEVILLE	●	●	●	●	●					●	
4	ALL MAJORCA	●	●	●	●	●						
5	ALL THE COSTA BRAVA	●	●	●	●	●						
6	ALL MALAGA and the Costa del Sol	●	●	●	●	●						
7	ALL THE CANARY ISLANDS(Gran Canaria).	●	●	●	●	●		●	●			
8	ALL CORDOBA	●	●	●	●	●					●	
9	ALL GRANADA	●	●	●	●	●		●			●	
10	ALL VALENCIA	●	●	●	●	●						
11	ALL TOLEDO	●	●	●	●	●					●	
12	ALL SANTIAGO	●	●	●	●	●						
13	ALL IBIZA and Formentera	●	●	●	●	●						
14	ALL CADIZ and the Costa de la Luz	●	●	●	●	●						
15	ALL MONTSERRAT	●	●	●	●	●	●					
16	ALL SANTANDER and Cantabria	●	●	●	●							
17	ALL THE CANARY ISLANDS II (Tenerife)	●	●	●	●	●		●	●			●
20	ALL BURGOS	●	●	●	●	●						
21	ALL ALICANTE and the Costa Blanca	●	●	●	●	●		●				
22	ALL NAVARRA	●	●	●	●							
23	ALL LERIDA	●	●	●	●		●					
24	ALL SEGOVIA	●	●	●	●	●						
25	ALL SARAGOSSA	●	●	●	●	●						
26	ALL SALAMANCA	●	●	●	●	●				●		
27	ALL AVILA	●	●	●	●	●						
28	ALL MINORCA	●	●	●	●	●						
29	ALL SAN SEBASTIAN and Guipúzcoa	●										
30	ALL ASTURIAS	●	●	●								
31	ALL LA CORUNNA and the Rías Altas	●	●	●	●							
32	ALL TARRAGONA	●	●	●	●	●	●					
33	ALL MURCIA	●	●	●	●							
34	ALL VALLADOLID	●	●	●	●							
35	ALL GIRONA	●	●	●	●							
36	ALL HUESCA	●	●									
37	ALL JAEN	●	●	●	●							
40	ALL CUENCA	●	●	●	●							
41	ALL LEON	●	●	●	●							
42	ALL PONTEVEDRA, VIGO and the Rías Bajas.	●	●	●	●							
43	ALL RONDA	●	●	●	●	●						
44	ALL SORIA	●		●								
46	ALL EXTREMADURA	●										
47	ALL ANDALUSIA	●	●	●	●	●						
52	ALL MORELLA	●	●		●		●					

Collection ALL AMERICA

		Spanish	French	English	German	Italian	Catalan	Dutch	Swedish	Portuguese	Japanese	Finnish
1	PUERTO RICO	●		●								
2	SANTO DOMINGO	●		●								
3	QUEBEC		●	●								
4	COSTA RICA	●		●								
5	CARACAS	●		●								

Collection ALL AFRICA

		Spanish	French	English	German	Italian	Catalan	Dutch	Swedish	Portuguese	Japanese	Finnish
1	MOROCCO	●	●	●	●	●						
2	THE SOUTH OF MOROCCO	●	●	●	●	●						
3	TUNISIA		●	●	●	●						
4	RWANDA		●									

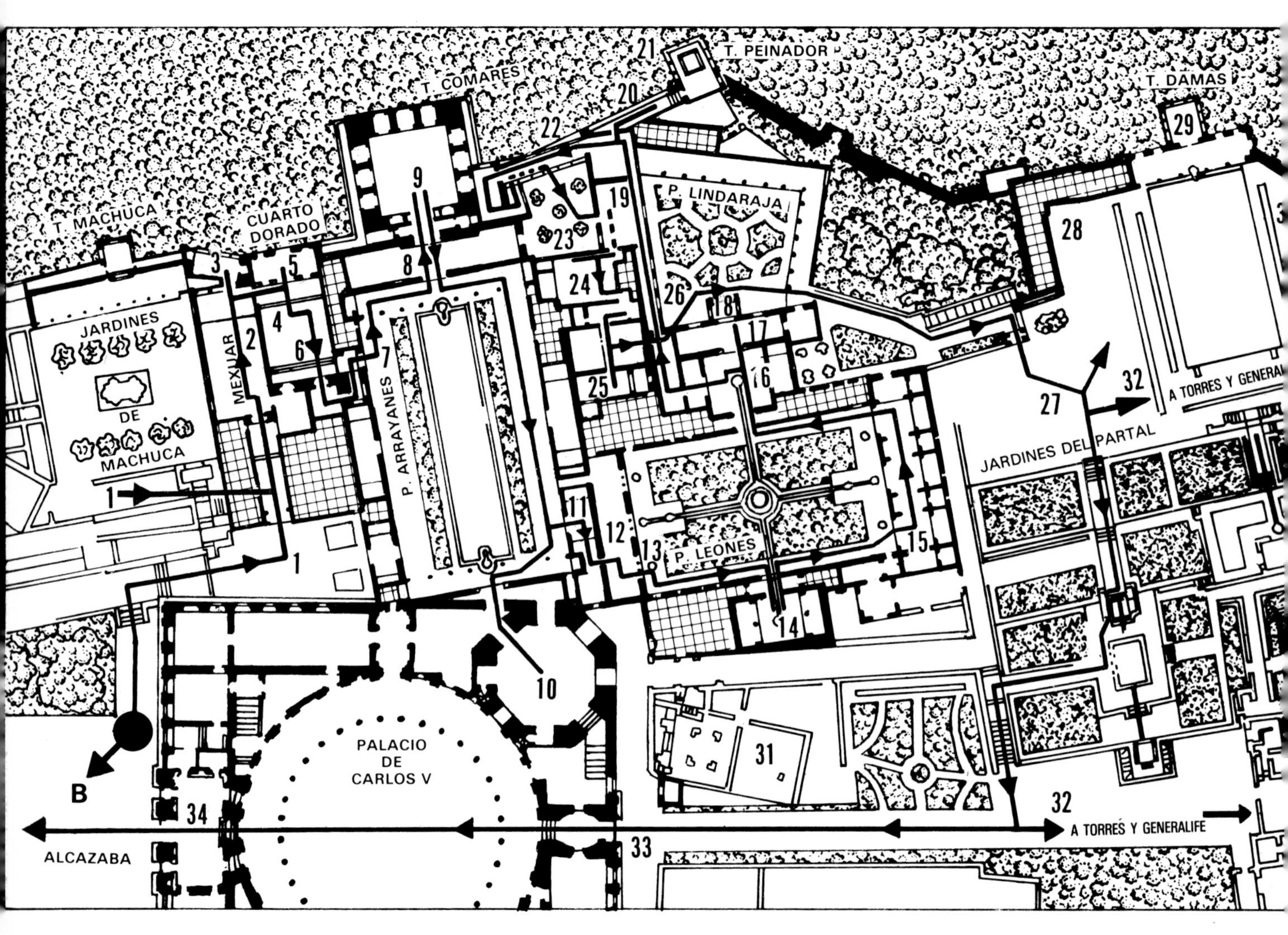

The Royal Palaces

B. Entrance tickets
1. Mexuar entrance
2. Mexuar chamber
3. Oratory
4. Mexuar court
5. Golden Room
6. Serrallo Palace entrance
7. Court of the Myrtle Trees
8. Barca gallery
9. Hall of the Ambassadors' (Comares Tower)
10. Chapel of Charles V's Palace
11. Harem entrance
12. Mocárabes gallery
13. Court of Lions
14. Abencerrajes gallery
15. Kings' chamber
16. Hall of the Two Sisters
17. Ajimeces gallery
18. Mirador of Lindaraja
19. Charles V's apartments
20. Gallery of the Mirador
21. Queen's boudoir
22. Corridor of columns
23. Cypress court
24. Rest room
25. Baths
26. Lindaraja garden
27. Partal gardens
28. Arab houses
29. Ladies' Tower
30. Mihrab Tower
31. Arab cemetery
32. Entrance to Towers and Generalife
33. Charles V's Palace
34. Exit and entrance to Alcazaba

5th Edition
I.S.B.N. 84-378-0956-8
Dep. Legal B. 1566-2000